# The New Way
# of
# Doing Business

## Jason Bertalli

B N R PARTNERS

Published by BNR Partners Pty Ltd ABN 85 354 278 697

Level 1, 327-333 Police Road, Mulgrave Victoria 3170

Phone (03) 9781 6800

www.bnrpartners.com.au

Copyright 2016 BNR Partners.

# Table of Contents

The New Way of Doing Business

# 1

## About the Author

Jason Bertalli was born and bred in a small town in country Victoria, moved to the "big smoke" of Melbourne to study science, changed to accounting, and is currently the Director of Franchise & Business Services at BNR Partners. He describes his current role as "meeting interesting people for coffee and helping them find solutions to their business problems". When not drinking coffee, he hits the pavement and the gym to try to keep up with his super fit wife and ever-active daughter and son.

THE **NEW WAY**
of
**DOING BUSINESS**

# 2

## Introduction

*"The Only Thing That Is Constant Is Change -". — Heraclitus*

There was a time, in the not so distant past that running a business seemed easy. If you were good at your trade, you eventually set off on your own, built up a customer base, hired some staff and ran your business. This organic growth model has worked very well for a lot of people. In some cases, it still does. But for most industries today, it is no longer so easy.

With the advent of the computer and the subsequent internet, efficiencies in transport (both local and international) and communication, and the general pace of life in western society increasing, a successful business today is not always reflective of its past. Some of the biggest businesses today are based on industries that did not exist not so long ago (Google was not a word I learnt at school, but we did eat Apples!) and some of the giants of yesteryear have long since gone to dust (we also used Kodak film back then...)

There is also the issue of small business failure. According to the Australian Bureau of Statistics, this rate could be higher than 60% within the first 3 years, not good odds by any stretch. The predominant reasons for this are not new concepts, however, with the leading issues being lack of capital, lack of strategy or simply a bad business idea.

So how do you make a go of a business today? What is the New Way of Doing Business?

The New Way of Doing Business is a concept that we have developed over the last 15 years of advising over 300 businesses, and is in short a process of taking all the ideas and actions that worked well, and proactively avoiding the ideas and actions that consistently led to negative issues. The thoughts and methods are not new, but are consistently underemployed to the detriment of most business operators.

Based on this, we encourage people to run a business on purpose. What this means is planned activity with a definitive goal in mind. Have a strategy that is actually thought out and documented. Refer to it when a decision is required – "How will this decision get me closer to the goals I set?" – and consciously run the business in the right direction. Heading aimlessly down a path, making "off the hip" decisions, is no longer a viable option for most business owners. The competition is too tough to allow forgiveness for those who err.

This does not mean that it is so rigid that no changes can be made to the direction of the business. Conversely, it allows decisions to be made on a conscious level to maximise opportunities. So how can this happen?

By using appropriate tools, keeping a sharp eye on the current state of the business and external environment, and consulting regularly with independent advisors to ensure that the business remains as dynamic as the industry it operates. Being able to react to changes as and when they occur, to minimise risk and ensure the best return on resources. Working to your strengths, whilst having a conscious awareness of your weaknesses. Perhaps most importantly, not being too proud to ask for help. There are countless examples of businesses that could have weathered the storm, had they received the right advice in a timely manner, instead of the owners ego pushing the "next deal will get us through" mentality. Note that if you ever think or say this, reach out immediately for professional assistance!

*"Only when the tide goes out do you discover who has been swimming naked"* **Warren Buffet**

As a business advisor for over 15 years, I have witnessed the acceleration of change to businesses and what they need to do to survive. In the good times, its parties and smiles all round, but as the above quote from Warren Buffet suggests, the true test of your business is when the economic tide turns and you need to draw on your reserves, both financial and resilience. The GFC was a turning point in this process, as was the Dot.com crash prior to this. The businesses that survived, or even flourished, during the aftermath of these events were those that realised the current way of operating was no longer working, and realised that they must adapt or die. This adaption by successful businesses, in a wide variety of industry and life cycle stages, has helped lead to our documenting and developing the New Way of Doing Business.

# 3

## What's the Secret?

Ok, so what is this secret sauce, this New Way of Doing Business? Time for a confession - to quote Mr Ping (Po's duck father in Kung Fu Panda) "The secret ingredient is....nothing!!! There is no secret ingredient" And so, there is nothing "new" in The New Way of Doing Business.

But before you throw this book away (or delete it if reading e-book style...), fear not, all is not lost.

The New Way of Doing Business is a concept. It is the application of a structured suite of thoughts and tools, readily available to all business owners, and assembling the parts to create a much bigger whole. The impact is in the synergy of many small, but vital, considerations, all applied with thought to enhance the business as compared to the competitors.

It is based on being "in the moment" and focused when considering the future direction of your business.

It involves being deliberate in how you plan, structure and execute business decisions to ensure they achieve the desired outcomes.

It is being nimble enough to react to external forces and seize opportunities.

It is about utilising resource pools to enhance your own businesses abilities and cover any shortcomings.

It is about sourcing the latest information and having the ability to interpret and implement this information in a structured way.

It is being confident enough in your message to tell all and sundry what you can do to help them solve their problems.

It is about being aware that we now operate on a global scale, no matter our business, and using this to our advantage.

It is about framing your business skills correctly to maximise your benefits.
It is also about what not to do.

It is not about paying the latest marketing guru thousands every month to be at the top of Google.

It is not about abdicating all responsibility and lying on a beach counting your millions. Yet, anyhow…

It is not about turning your business on its ear on day one to fix everything at once.

This book will step out a framework of how to consider, construct and implement the steps needed to keep you at the front of the pack, remain ahead of your competitors and run your business using The New Way of Doing Business methodology.

But first things first, let's get some hard to swallow home truths out of the road.

Penetrating question 1 – why do you think you deserve a successful business?

The cold hard truth? Many if not most small business owners do not deserve a successful business. Bit rough? Maybe. But consider this- a bad business owner will stumble along, selling enough widgets to pay some of the bills, but most likely will go backwards just quickly enough to rack up huge debts to the likes of the ATO, the major suppliers and most likely a bank or two. One day, they finally join the way too large percentage of SME business failures in this country, having enjoyed more lifestyle than they paid for, at the expense of everybody else. If society is lucky, they go broke and go get a job somewhere. If not, they start another venture under the protection of the corporate veil and the whole sideshow begins again.

The effect of the above on the cost of labour, the cost of "stuff" and the general cost of doing business is substantial. So apology for the soapbox rant, but no, not everyone should be in business. If you are buying yourself a job, save the rest of us the pain and just get a job. If, however, you really want to make a dent in the universe through successfully building a stable and viable business, then society should back you every step of the way.

Rant over.

So, you have kept reading and nothing above twinged a guilt nerve? Congrats, let's see what you need!

Assuming you don't already own a business, do you now buy an established business or set up a greenfield, a brand new business from scratch? Do you buy/start an independent or a franchise? What is your financial position? How much will you need? Are you adequately experienced or will you need training in some or all aspects? Is your goal to get rich or follow your passion? Is your longer term plan to keep or sell the business?

Generate an income stream or build and "flip" for a quick capital gain?

All valid and vitally important questions, and for the most part beyond the scope of this text and adequately covered in dedicated titles in most every bookshop – and Amazon search – so have a ponder if needed, and either stop here and revisit, or move on with us now. I'm happy either way. Actually, it's a book, I will never know! Just promise yourself that if these aren't covered in your mind, ensure that you do. Elements we cover later will bring this stuff to the fore anyhow.

In order to help the visuals reading this book, the format we will follow will be that we cover a concept or small selection of concepts, and then show how these have been applied in the real world. I figured the best way to do this is to follow the journey of a business, and a business person, from the basic old school style of operation, of doing a good job and getting paid, through the change process of fine tuning the business to a machine that provides a planned and structured outcome. It is not a perfect example, as in the real world, there is no perfect example. But it is an example of what can be achieved by the application of the overarching principles outlined in this book.

So let's meet our example. Let's meet Joe the Entrepreneur.

# The New Way of Doing Business

# 4

## Meet Joe the Entrepreneur

Joe is the sort of bloke you would expect to meet at the pub or at a mate's BBQ. He grew up middle class in a nice neighbourhood, went to public school and had a relatively normal upbringing. A moderately smart kid, he completed Year 11 before leaving to begin his apprenticeship as a plumber.

The shining star of his local footy team, he was always popular and as such a job was not hard to find. He progressed through the ranks at his employer, the largest plumbing business in the area, to site supervisor before questioning in his own mind the future career path if he stayed on. The boss' business was big, but stagnant, offering limited scope for him past his current role and the occasional pay rise to keep up with inflation. So after much pondering and discussing with the wife, Joe began the process of heading out on his own, and eventually started Joe's Plumbing (obviously named by his mates one Friday after work)

The initial few years were a bit tight, with Joe taking a serious pay cut as he set up his own clientele and built a reputation for reliability and quality work. Fast forward to the present, though and Joe, now 34, built up the business to now employing 6 staff and turning over just shy of $2m pa. This provides Joe and his family (wife and two kids, son 8 and daughter 5) with a comfortable lifestyle, with plenty of long weekends to enjoy his toys and the occasional overseas holiday.

However, over the last few years Joe has noticed things getting a bit tougher in the market.

Some of the quotes for building development jobs in the area have been getting costed below what Joe can currently compete with. Having done some reverse maths, some jobs even seem to be losing money for the winning tender to get across the line.

Some of Joe's smaller but regular clients are getting basic quotes online from a mobile plumbing mob now operating in the area.

There are definitely more of these "other mob" vans around now than there used to be.

While Joe is still making a good living, he can see the writing on the wall – if he doesn't do something, this lifestyle will take an unpleasant adjustment south!

But what does he need to do? Where does he start? At the beginning is as good a place as any.....

# The New Way of Doing Business

# 5

## Business on Purpose

The idea of doing business on purpose is not new; I'm sure you have heard of companies having strategy days, setting forward forecasts and having regular budgeting meetings. Businesses have always had visions, missions and value statements. Staff culture is not a new phenomenon.

What is new is the size of businesses and the time in their business cycle that the successful businesses are implementing these "big business" ideals into their own. There are a few reasons for this.

### Banks

In the not so distant past, a business owner made an appointment with his bank manager, donned some clean clothes and sat down with the last years financials to discuss the overdraft required to keep the business operational. The manager had a quick glance, punched some basic numbers into a computer and authorised the appropriate amount based on his assessment.

The process today is slightly more involved. Whilst it is still important to have a relationship with your manager, perhaps more so than previously, of greater significance is the reporting that the bank will require in order to help your business out.

Today, you will need your historical information, preferably updated to at least the last financial quarter, as well as forecast budgets with profit /loss and balance sheet, forward cash flow projections and capex requirements.

The good news? These tools are what you will need to begin your business on purpose journey. The bad news? You will need these now to begin your business on purpose journey!

**The ATO**

Since 2000, all businesses have been (or more correctly, have been required to be...) reporting interim financial data to the Australian Taxation Office Depending on the scale of your business – turnover, employees, tax liability – this could be as often as monthly. Whilst at first seeming an onerous burden on the busy business owner, we have seen this as forced introduction to business improvement, as never before has there been such a focus on knowing your numbers.

The analytics that this data provides is a double edged sword though. On one hand, having a business focus on, or at least prepare, the reporting necessary has created a great awareness of performance, and also allowed access to much better data for things such as benchmarking and trend analysis.

The flip side is that it has allowed the ATO greater access to much better data such as benchmarking and trend analysis. Audit activity is now easier and more successful (from the ATO's point of view) than it has ever been due to the amount of data and the analysis using ever increasing computing power. If you are operating an old school business, or taking some cash on the side, it's almost a given that the ATO will be in touch soon.

**Computing Power**

*Moore's Law –"Overall processing power for computers will double every two years"*

The level and speed with which computing power, and the related adaption of cloud based computing, has developed, and subsequently has been embraced by the business community, is astounding. Computers that would have been the envy of big businesses only 10 years ago are now surpassed by phones in the pocket of most teenagers, and being implemented for such value adding activities as snapchat and PokemonGo. We now have an upcoming generation that don't believe life existed before the iPhone, or that televisions once had buttons for channel selection. Whilst a constant source of fear and scepticism for some, for most it has opened up opportunities in business that could not have been dreamed of by previous generations. Who would have thought that your accounting software would talk to your point of sale software, reconciled with your stock control and HR add-ons, imported and reconciled automatic bank feeds and give you an accurate 24/7 view of your business, current to the minute, on your phone?

From an advisor's point of view this is awesome. We can have a constant monitoring of clients positions, and be in touch if anything looks unusual, allowing almost instant attention to problems that may not have previously been attended for weeks, months or even at all previously.

**Big Data**

Much is being said about the concept of big data, and its potential effect on not only our business lives, but on life in general. So what is big data? In my own simplistic view, big data is simply masses of information that are now actually useful due to the increases in computing power, from both a cost and speed/capacity point of view. As computer processing improves exponentially, so does our ability to collate, sort and analyse huge volumes of data to come to practical assumptions on future results. For example, being able to review the entire purchasing process of something like eBay or amazon gives new insights into online shopping behaviour. Facebook, to my mind the most awesome data collection point ever and also the scariest, provides almost unlimited abilities for analysis of basic human behaviours of every element from who reads what when to who goes where and why.

Could this technology be applied to your business to help you understand your customers and maybe focus of helping them better? Most likely.

Of course, there are still items needing attending to make sense of this data. You guessed it – budgets, forecast cash flows and benchmarks are all needed to measure against.

So how do we set these financial and other indicators? Again, it starts at the beginning, with a strategy.

**Strategy**

*"Would you tell me, please, which way I ought to go from here?"*
*"That depends a good deal on where you want to get to."*
*"I don't much care where –"*
*"Then it doesn't matter which way you go."*

**Lewis Carroll, Alice in Wonderland**

So why are you in business? Why are you in this business? What do you sell, and to who? Where do you find them, and when is the best time to deal with them? How do you find them? Are you doing what you are best at, and getting rewarded accordingly?

The setting of a strategic plan for your business is essential to not only answer the above questions, but to ensure that you are making the best use of the resources you have to hand.

So what is a strategic plan? It is a road map for your business upon which you can refer for assistance in making decisions that will affect your business. It is as simple as that. Is it a fixed, set-and -forget style document? Unfortunately for some it is. There are times of frustration when, asked if they have a strategic plan for the business, the business owners proudly drag out a dust covered tomb prepared years ago, most likely by an overpriced consultant. When asked, no-one has any idea what the contents actually contain! This is not a strategic plan; it is an expensive and mostly useless platitude from the board to management to feign proactivity.

A true strategy is well thought out, understood and communicated. It is also referenced and updated regularly to ensure its relevance to the business and the business' place in the bigger scheme of things.

This book is not a definitive guide to setting a strategy for your business. There are plenty of dedicated resources available to cover this area in much more detail than I do here. What we will do however is step through a helicopter view of setting a strategic direction, and who better than Joe's Plumbing to lead us through the process.

**Joe's Strategic Journey**

"Joe, we need to sit down and map out some future direction for your business"

"I'm too busy to worry about that sort of stuff, can't you just do it for me and send me the bill?"

"As inviting as printing out a templated strategic plan with your name on it for a fee sounds, this is not how the process works. I'll get you booked in for a ½ day starter next week"

And so begins the turnaround process for Joe's Plumbing. He did turn up, and we set down some guidance on how to create an effective strategy for the future of his business. First, we defined what a strategy should achieve. It was to guide us from point A, where we are now, to point B, which is the notional end point.

In Joe's case, he is only young and has a young family, so his goals were his and his alone. His point B was originally to hand the business down to his kids, but that is many years away. In all seriousness, a parent wishing to hand a business to their children who are 5 and 8 is optimistic at best – will there even be plumbers by then? Will we have dedicated handy-robots? Who knows? So we needed a closer star to shoot at, setting the time frame for 5 years.

Joe stated in 5 years, he wants to take his family on a 3-month extended vacation to Africa, in order to expose his kids to a more diversified view of the world, and bond as a family before the kids "hit high school, graduate and leave home" (apparently a 6-year integrated process that seems to last 50 years for the child and 22 seconds for the parent)

So from here, we start digging. How much will that cost? Who will run the business? Will you need to be contactable 24/7 or can it be left alone for that long? What do you need to generate, over and above your living needs, to support this trip? We started to get a bit of a picture of what life in 5 years look like for Joe. Now, we needed to look at what we currently had, and then map the journey.

Joe had a current team of 6 employees. The team runs as a group of mates, with a collegiate style respect and obligation to each other. This has served well, and is a strength that Joe can capitalise on.

With a turnover of around $2m, and a net margin of 20%, Joe was doing ok financially. But he was worried about sustainability of this.

The issues were the pressure building to sharpen his quotes, and the growing online plumber presence in his local area.

Time for some more crystal balling. Joe needed to visualise what he saw the business as in 5 years, taking in to conscious consideration the factors above.

He came up with the following:

- Staff of 10, with a turnover of $3.6 m (based on $300k month)
- Maintain margin of 20% net profit
- Some sort of online marketing that's competing with the current online plumbers
- A good reputation as the reliable blokes to get the job done

This is when I asked him "How does this fit within the business' vision longer term, and tie in with your mission statement?"

"You're going to make me do this stuff now too, aren't you?"

"Yes, Joe"

He looked down, looked up and smiled in resignation. Which was a relief. I thought he was going to hit me.

## Vision and Mission Statements

Not so long ago even I believed that vision and mission statements were simply feel good outcome statements used by marketers to justify their existence. Big listed companies had them, usually full of motherhood terms and grandiose global goals, stuck up on the wall behind reception and usually forgotten by staff in general.

But as the title of this book suggests, there is now a New Way of Doing Business. Smaller business can now compete with bigger business much easier. This more-level playing field gives advantages, but you need to know what tools are required. These tools now include having a solid vision and mission for your business that is clearly and easily communicated. If it's easier for more people to see your business, you better make sure that what they see is the right message, designed by you. It's the old story, if you don't stand for something, people assume you stand for nothing.

These statements are important on a number of levels. With more access and transparency now, your business has potential to be exposed on a wider range of stakeholders than ever before.

It's important to customers, who can gain an insight into your business without direct contact by simply seeing your vision and mission (and values, which is next!). You only get one chance to make a first impression, and as that is often your website as potential clients anonymously compare you to your competition, it better show them who you really are.

It's important to your suppliers, who as you would expect like to know who they are dealing with. More and more, suppliers are researching their customers online for clues on trading history, issues with other suppliers and other titbits to see who you are and if they can trust you as a customer.

And it's massively important to your staff. If they know where the business is and where it is planning on heading, they can take comfort in securing their future with you. Or not, as they case may be if there is a cultural misfit. Either way, this is a good thing for overall culture and staff morale.

So what's the difference between a vision and a mission? Many confuse these terms, and a quick search online will reveal numerous large companies that seem to have crossbred these terms to somehow get to some interesting results. In the end, this is not a deal breaker, but the message that they convey is – you need to share these to enable true leadership and to maximise buy in form staff and other stakeholders.

Again, there are volumes based on just this topic, but for the purpose of simplicity I define them as

Mission – What we do, who for, and how. In other words, why the business exists, our reason for being.

Vision – the end goal, where we want to end up.

## So Back to Joe

Without taking you through the entire process thought by thought, Joe and I sat with a marketing contact of mine and two of Joe's key staff and they came up with the following:

*Vision:* "To be the plumbers of first choice for the domestic and commercial building industry in our local area"

Nice, neat, easy to recall and some bones they can hang some meat on. Is it perfect? Maybe, maybe not. But it's there and it's theirs.

*Mission:* "We solve your plumbing needs on time and on budget, with quality materials and expert tradespeople"

Again, not the most eloquent of statements, but it was built around what the business currently does, how they do it, and who they do it for. It focuses on the pain points of potential customers, and suggests how they attend to those needs. To that end, it's close enough and effective in its message.

Best of all, these two statements of where we are and where we want to be can be our guiding light for the previously discussed operational strategy, giving much needed clarity and comfort to Joe through this process. We had broken the back of it finally, and it should get easier from here.

"So what's next? "asked Joe, who has by now worked out that every step leads him to another unknown piece of the business puzzle.

"Values, Joe. We need to articulate the core business values to fully flesh out the personality of the business"

"Seriously" he murmurs "didn't even know it needed its own personality."

**Core Values**

Core values are the guiding principles that are used internally in a business to guide decision making and behaviours. The advantage is that your business is already operating with a subconscious set of core values that will be evidenced by your underlying corporate culture. So as long as the base culture of your business is what you would like it to be, this process is simply a discovery process. If however your culture is not ideal, or is even heading toward toxic, then work needs to be done to both set and enforce the values that you wish to see held by your business.

Values are another of those areas that are looked upon as superficial and a waste of time by many small business owners (and big business, too). Again, as per the vision and mission, the worth of having carefully articulated values that are a true indication of the culture of your business can be harder to measure but provide a valuable competitive advantage in this new transparent and accessible world. It is another vital element in the New Way of Doing Business, and is important is some key areas such as interviewing for a new position, integrating new staff to the business, or developing an elevator pitch that truly reflects your business.

Joe was lucky. His business already had a healthy culture, based on a friendly "group of mates" style of operation. The issue was how to keep this culture strong in the face of growth and change. This is why he needed to articulate what he had, so any new staff, customers or other stakeholders would immediately view his business through the correct cultural lens.

Sitting down with his whole team, and with guidance, the process began with a chat about what the team valued, what they thought the clients valued, and what was perceived internally to give the business its "presence" in the market.

After much discussion and fine tuning (this is not a process to gloss over in an hour over lunch!) they came up with the following:

- Always Professional
  - This carried on from dressing neatly and removing shoes at the clients' door, to how tidy the toolboxes and work vehicles are kept, to using manners and being courteous at all times. Not a rough swearing bloke with the traditional plumber's crack for example!
- Embrace the New

- o Always be looking for ways to improve, be that the customer experience, latest methods and materials, or tools and software to make life easier
- Be Reliable
  - o This was to reflect both internally and externally – do what you say you are going to do, when you said you would, or at least communicate why not as early as possible
- Have Fun
  - o The culture is based on a close knit group, and they often socialised together or with each other separately. The team decided that this made a difference in how they worked and how they were perceived by clients, so it made the cut

Whilst not rocket science, these four values could now be used to guide how the business looked and felt going forward. They give guidance to the team, help Joe to articulate how his business operates, and give a solid base to set the future direction of the business.

So it was now time to revisit the previous strategy notes and test them for fit.

**Glue it Together**

Recall how Joe had come up with some ideas on the business at the 5-year mark? They were:

- Staff of 10, with a turnover of $3.6 m (based on $300k month)
- Maintain margin of 20% net profit

- Some sort of online marketing that's competing with the current online plumbers
- A good reputation as the reliable blokes to get the job done

Joe now needed to work these over a bit more, and tie them together with the business' vision, mission and values statements to get a crystal clear picture of what they had and what they were going to aim for. This was discussed and then parked for a future date, as Joe deemed other issues pending as priority and wanted to "settle what we had already "and there were no obvious conflicting issues.

# 6

## Jack Be Nimble

*"In the new world, it is not the big fish that eats the small fish, it's the fast fish that eats the slow fish"* Klaus Schwab, World Economic Forum

The world is changing fast. That's why you are reading this book. The global economy is reflecting success for being fast to act, and even faster to react. You need only look to companies such as Uber, who created a massive business getting people to use their own cars, and Airbnb, same story with peoples spare space, to see that being a massive conglomerate is now not the only way to become a world leader, and may even hinder your future performance. So how do they do it? In a big part, by being nimble.

The typical big business model that came to mind until recently would usually involve an office or group of offices, with teams of people on the books, working 9-5 to ensure that the widgets get from idea to customer through "the machine".

The machine could involve product development, logistics, marketing, HR, accounting, IT and a myriad of other teams, all with their own goals and objectives, most likely controlled by a management level and overseen by a board of directors.

Decision making would be stifled at best, and an idea to grab an opportunity by turning the big ship 5 degrees left would involve a protracted array of meetings and evaluation committees and the like, until eventually the command comes to turn 15 degrees right.

Then along came, amongst other factors, the internet. All of the sudden, by the time big business turned the ship, all the customers were being catered for by the new wave of smaller competitors in speed boats! Each level of the process had been tweaked, with communication, sourcing, marketing, every element being cheaper, easier and quicker than it ever had before.

Now you are thinking "but I have a small business, how does this affect me?"

The next stage came when bigger businesses also utilised these new resources and restructured to suit. They eventually turned left 5 degrees. With efficiency and increased speed, the little clients that were not commercially viable to supply previously are now able to deal direct via technology solutions with bigger businesses. These may be your current or potential clients!

So what do we do? How can we compete with these heavily resourced companies? Be nimble.

There are a mind blowing number of alternative solutions to business problems today. Can't afford to rent an office? Join a cooperative workspace. Don't have internet? Buy a coffee at your local and use theirs, its most likely free. Can't afford a full time PA but need some help with the admin? Hire a Virtual Assistant. (Note - If you can get your head around most roles in your business being task based as opposed to an all-encompassing job package, it's easy to allocate the tasks)

Really, there is nothing that can't be done quicker, easier and cheaper than it previously had. Having less is now more.

The secret sauce is to design your business and then break down what you need, and source the most flexible and viable solution to suit your needs. Less is more, and if can satisfy the needs of your target market with a nimble scalable model, isn't that what it is really all about?

Now depending on your business you may need a physical location, or a team of full time employees, or a high bandwidth dedicated internet connection, and if that is the case then that's fine. What is important, though, is that you need to be aware of the options available and you need to be brutally honest about what is required to run your business

So how does this apply to Joe? To figure this out, we needed to find the current status first.

Joe had a good business, but it was old school in that it was very manual in operation and relied too much on people. To schedule jobs, Joe had to remember what was going on weeks in advance, until he got back to the office to check his whiteboard. Quotes were done in a quote book, and then entered onto the computer to send the quote by email (this was forced by the builders more than foresight!) and saved in a folder titled "quotes" on the desktop. Once a week, the bookkeeper would drive out to his place and sit for a few hours entering bills and invoices onto his computer and reconcile the latest bank statements. Most bills were paid on time using Joe's credit card, and these were also tracked correctly assuming he used the right one!

When clients called, they either used Joe's mobile (most common) or the office number that usually went to an answering machine and he would call back later.

Joe had a website, the result of "some bloke peddling a solution in a box, but took the cash and ran...", resulting in a one pager that at least had an email address and phone number (see answering machine above!)

So let's say that the machine wasn't exactly fine-tuned yet. First things first, the business needed to be nimble (in terms of responsive). So what did we decide?

There were several tools to make life much, much easier for Joe and the team. The list for the short term included the following solutions.

- IPads were bought for all vehicles, and these were loaded with some pretty cool and easy to use software.
- The software was used to schedule jobs using cloud technology, so all iPads synchronised together and everybody knew what everyone else was doing. Joe could send the guys home in the van the night before, and they didn't even need to come to the office first, saving hours of non-productive time. A no brainer.
- It also allowed for quoting to be done on site, and then synced with the workflow to allow indicative scheduling for the client
- This quote talked to the accounting software, creating an invoice and allowing it to be emailed from the vehicle. Quotes were being spec'd, authorised and sent immediately from the iPad by Joe, and some clients even accepted and paid electronically on the spot!

Joe also moved from desktop to cloud accounting software, paying a monthly service to allow automatic bank feeds of all accounts and credit cards. His bookkeeper could now access the file remotely, saving an hour of travel (that Joe was paying for) and giving a much more timely and accurate account of how the business was travelling.

We appointed a new IT consulting business, who as well as arranging the iPads and software setups, reviewed and quoted to update the website.

- The look was modernised to bring it into this century
- An enquiry page was set up, to allow email enquiries and well as phone.
- Some keywords were used to help improve the local SEO results.
- Content was loaded that reflected our vision and mission, our values, and a resultant service level statement that would give potential clients additional comfort.

It was decided that having an email enquiry was no good unless the response rate increased, and a solution for that was to engage a remote service to respond to emails. This service, using staff in the Philippines, was also set up to answer the work phone on diversion after 4 rings, and we added a popup "can we help you" on the website because, well, we could as they were responding to phone and email anyhow.

This all added up to give Joe a massive presence, as at any time he could take an enquiry, respond quickly (the iPads gave the ability to GPS track the vehicles live) and engage the client in a much more efficient way, and have the comfort that he wasn't overpromising and under delivering.

Was this the perfect solution? No

It took the guys a while to get used to the software.

There were coding errors that flowed through to the accounting software and caused GST issues.

Some staff weren't that keen on being tracked.

In sorting the auto answer on the website, the responses sometimes weren't in "Joe speak" and some regulars made comment on using slave labour and costing Aussie jobs.

Oh, and Joe quoted the same job 3 times in one day, accidentally, and had to buy the client lunch after conceding to the lowest quote….

But overall it went ok, the system once settled definitely improved the flow of work, overtime was reduced even though sales increased (mostly saved in travel), and the boys seemed at peace with the growth. They were even winning jobs from online enquiries occasionally.

Joe was not yet the Uber of plumbing, or the Airbnb of fixing your pipes, but in his industry, he had definitely moved his way to the pointy end of the boat. He was now reaping the rewards with what overall had been a relatively easy and cost effective process. He felt responsive for the first time in years. He felt nimble.

The New Way of Doing Business

# 7

## Collaboration Beats Competition, Hands Down

*"Competition makes us faster; Collaboration makes us better!"*
*Unknown*

What would you say if I told you the best way to improve your business was to sit down in a closed room, with your competitors, and talk strategy about how to deal with various internal and external industry issues?

Put like that, most people have a first response along the lines of looking at their watch, finishing their coffee quickly and attempting to politely excuse themselves while planning excuses to not return my calls or pay my invoice.

But stick with me, even if with suspended disbelief, for a little longer.

We are living in an age where privacy is all but an illusion. Your iPhone tracks your movements, your computer remembers what you searched for last week, and Facebook can recognise you in someone else's photo. Do you really think that your competition doesn't know what you're up to?

So with that clarified, what better way than to team up with some competitors (ok, a gentle start, maybe not direct competitors but other industry participants) and throw some ideas around.

Please note, I am not talking about price fixing or market manipulation here, but simply finding a solution to a common problem using other people's experiences and results. It is a more common approach than you think. Many industries have discussion group style arrangements where you can participate to the level you are comfortable with, and most likely take away some real value.

Another option is a professional network group, such as EO or TEC, where you can regularly rub shoulders with a variety of other business owners from a range of industries and share strategies that have worked, or not, mostly in a safe environment using Chatham House rules or a similar honour system of privacy and respect.

A more personal touch can be obtained by finding yourself a mentor. Some may be surprised that successful high level business people, who may seem unobtainable for a meeting or to pitch an idea, are often agreeable to the idea of forming a mentor relationship and helping a less experienced business person with their knowledge and experience. The thought of giving back and helping someone avoid the mistakes they may have encountered on their journey is often a feel good that can add value not only to the mentored, but also the mentor themselves.

So Joe and I sat for a chat.

"I don't know anyone who I can hook up with in my industry, and will I really have time for all this once the internet sends all these leads?"

"Listen Joe, firstly the business is running better than it ever has, and you aren't as involved, so yes you'll make the time. Second, if you don't get feedback and advice outside your comfort zone, you will not grow, either business or personally, to anywhere near your capability."

We decided on Joe joining EO, as well as attending more industry events and supplier networking engagements.

The process with EO, where the focus is on personal, business and family, would be just what Joe needed to gain some life perspective and a wider view of the world. The exposure to a new group of people would show Joe that he can be different to the other suburban plumbers. He has some great ideas tucked away, apparently, so with a bit of confidence and the access to the right tools, this could be an exciting path forward.

Through Joe's industry activities, he ended up sitting on the state guidance committee, and was now also talking regular with the plumbing industry movers and shakers. The ability to get a global perspective, and see what was coming from around the world, would allow Joe to keep ahead of the curve and maintain a competitive advantage.

Joe also sent a couple of boys to join some BNI groups, to not only secure leads, but to also groom them up for bigger roles in the company itself. Through the BNI process (which is in short a referral /lead swapping group) the guys had generated some jobs, but also secured some interesting advertising at discounted rates, and found a new apprentice.

Joe had turned from the doubtful outlook of impending competitive forces, to now looking to actually fulfilling the company vision and becoming "the plumbers of first choice for the domestic and commercial building industry in our local area"

Things were looking good.

# 8

## Knowledge is No Longer Power

Knowledge was power. Back in 1597, Sir Francis Bacon wrote *"ipsa scientia potestas est"*, translated as "knowledge itself is power". This was based on a principle of scarcity, as the knowledge was proprietary, not easily distributed on any scale, and relatively easy to keep under wraps. As discussed in the previous chapter, this is far from the case now. Times have changed, and most businesses and people in general, have an overload of knowledge.

Google, which was only listed in 2004, is not only one of the most valuable companies in the world, but has changed the information gathering and collating process entirely. In fact, no matter which search engine you use on the internet, you would most likely say you are going to Google it. Funnily, saying you are going to Bing or Yahoo something ends in strange looks!

So I defy anyone to suggest they actually know more than the information available on the internet. It's preposterous. So why would we therefore think that knowledge is still power. Want to know what power is now? Finding, sorting and implementing all that knowledge, that's power. IBM's Watson, currently the most powerful set of computers on the planet, would have been thought to be a valuable asset to be guarded closely and milked for its benefits. It's available now, to everyone.

Have a think about your own industry. Are you paid purely for what you know, based on a principal of scarcity to keep up the value proposition? Do you sell a product that is currently hard to source? Be very careful. A business built on scarcity, in an age where collaboration and global access is increasing at an amazing rate, may render your business model redundant in short order. I know for example that I wouldn't buy a taxi licence today, where they were a great asset until Uber hit the world. The taxi licence was limited in issue, so based on scarcity, it was valuable, with local licences here in Melbourne ranging around $500,000 each. That changed quickly. The current government is negotiating a buy back deal offering $100,000 for the first licence held, and less for subsequent licences, not such a good investment nowadays. So what is your value based on?

We put Joe through the paces with this in mind. What did the business do to create a value proposition, and was this based on knowledge or something else?

Any home handyperson can pop down to the local hardware store and get plumbing supplies. They could then Google a YouTube video of how to, for example, fix their toilet. After 3 trips to Bunnings and several half cooked sausages in bread, and most of the day gone, home handyperson may have finally managed to fix the problem.

Similar, with the construction jobs, and noting legal compliance issues are there but ignored for the sake of simplicity, the builder could lay his own pipes and run water where required. It would be a bit of trial and error to ensure that it all hooked up correctly and did what they wanted, but they could do it. They don't.

The reason both home handyperson and the project manager/builders use Joe's business is because his training and experience solves a scarcity issue for them and that is time. By applying the knowledge, by using experience, he saves time and effort.

The power is not in the knowing, but in the application of that knowledge. People will pay you to fix the problem, not to know how to fix the problem.

# 9

## Marketing – Shout it From the Rooftops

If you have read this far, you are most likely in the mindset of trying to improve your life and the life of your business. That's awesome, well done!

This chapter may challenge you, however, as most people have preconceived ideas about marketing and sales that are not necessarily helpful. First, let's try and define what the terms mean.

**My Definitions Are**:

*Sales:* - the one on one process of helping solve a problem using your product or service

*Marketing*: - a one to many process of raising awareness with your target market, to lead them to the sales process

So applying the definitions above, your business is probably already doing this in a fashion somewhere along the spectrum from crap to fantastic. Let's deconstruct the processes to see how you can do this better. Before we start, I will again reiterate that this book is an overview of the processes required to embrace the New Way of Doing Business. There is a plethora of information that drills down into the specific areas of sales and marketing, and I encourage you to seek this out and really broaden your view in this space.

Starting with sales, the basic skills have not really changed over the years. The ability to communicate clearly, articulate the value of your particular product or service, and help solve a problem for your client still cuts through. People still deal with people, and if they have a choice they will deal with people they like and trust.

What has changed is the way you communicate your persona to help enhance the speed and depth that you can create this level of connection and trust. The purchasing decision is now enhanced or assisted from the clients' point of view with much more accessible information to compare and review products and services. As with most aspects of our life, tech has accelerated change.

If you are a service provider, your potential customers may traditionally have come from a referral. This referral may have arranged to meet up with you, have a coffee and chat and evaluate your service offerings and determine whether they like or trust you from that meeting.

So what is different now? Well the client can still be referred, or may even check you out direct if your marketing is effective, but they will most likely not go from that first step direct to an appointment. There may well be added steps that can either help or hinder your chances of even getting to the meeting point. The client will google you. They will google your business and check out your website. They will look for any online reviews to reduce the decision resistance (people trust and believe independent reviews, even if they don't know the reviewer! Don't believe me? Check out sites like TripAdvisor....) They will watch your YouTube videos, listen to your podcasts, read your blogs, check any books you have written, and pull anything else that Google will present to them. If that presents a reasonable picture of you and your business, they may then arrange to either deal with you or meet to discuss options.

So having thought about this new process that the client does mostly without you even knowing they exist, do you really still consider marketing is simply setting a Yellow Pages advert and sponsoring the local netball club? What do you think your competitors are doing or starting to do? What would Joe do?

Well Joe was already partially aware of this beginning to affect his business. Remember he mentioned the increase in "the online mob's vans floating around"? So the first thing was to have a closer look and see who they were and what they were doing. Whilst copying the opposition is not a sure fire way to success, awareness is still necessary.

So we googled plumbing the local area. Guess what? This competitor had the first five spots covered. No wonder people were booking them, there was almost no choice. The good thing, though, is that there was almost no one else on the first page either, so the competition for ranking was still relatively low. Some smart SEO and planning for the social media strategy should provide some good results straight up.

So we sat down with an SEO advisor from the IT company we had appointed to map out our plan of attack. After consideration of Podcasts, blogs, YouTube, writing and promoting an e-book, promoting speaking gigs, Facebook, Instagram, Twitter, snapchat and some other platforms, it was decided to use the KISS principle and keep it simple stupid.

Most traffic would be generated from the website. So stage one, set the site accordingly. We already had an email responder, so once on the site we could handle the enquiry. We just had to get people there. That needed some smart SEO work. The quickest and easiest way to do that was to leverage from the best. If you google pretty much anything, the top sites that rank are usually YouTube, LinkedIn, Googles own (Google+, Google Maps, etc.) and sites with the right keywords, content and history. So, after registering the business with Google Maps (free) to show up on the google map search, it was time to review LinkedIn and YouTube.

Joe did a short video, explaining why the business was different (note that we had done this work during the strategy sessions, so all this is now starting to tie together) and ensuring the title was what his target customers would use to search for his services. It showed his personality, some of his staff and equipment, and walked around a very nice clean worksite. Perfect marketing for his target's clients.

Joe also did a quick video on how to fix a washer in a tap. This worked to both improve the spread of his marketing, and save him time from people calling to ask him how to do it!

We updated Joe's LinkedIn profile to include the business details, and focused on what he did for his target customers. Again, it's easy to focus when you have done the strategic work already, and this saved heaps of time and money once we arrived at this point. We also set up LinkedIn profiles for all of the staff, and Joe's wife, purely to enhance the chance of successful hits in a search. It also put a face to the names of the staff, allowing a more personal image to be portrayed.

All these touch points had links to the website, where visitors could be assisted by the help desk popup or contact the business via email or phone.

So what happened? In the beginning, not too much. But after a short while, something strange happened. People started giving Joe little jibes about being a movie star. Joking about getting his autograph in the pub, things like that. Not a huge amount, but enough that Joe noticed. So he rang the SEO guy to get a report.

"Joe, it's the funniest thing. To start with not much happened online, but during the long weekend, your video on how to fix a leaking tap went ballistic!"

Now it began to make sense. A long weekend, funnily enough, had created a spike in home handymen needing to fix a leaking tap. As Joe's video was titled perfectly, and was current, it had taken a heap of traffic. Not exactly the result we expected, but a bonus in the eyes of the Google-bots, so great for SEO. And apparently for Joe's reputation as a movie star too!

The thing with the internet is that no one has it sorted, so it can surprise the most experienced campaigners. I have a mate who made money with footage of when an eagle attacked his drone, the footage went viral and ended up on prime time TV in the US. Who'd have guessed? People are strange animals, trying to predict social behaviour is an art form at best.

This leads to another point with online marketing – measure it. There are some awesome tools and capabilities now to measure who visits your site, for how long, where they click, what stage they get to before they abandon your shopping cart, any action you can think of can be measured and managed. Ensure you do this as best as you can with consideration of course to your business model and strategy. If you are going to spend money online, ensure it is spent in the best possible way. There are still some rogue operators out there that will charge you a small fortune, promise you the earth, and come up light with results. With the tech available today, there is no excuse for them to try this on, or for you to accept mediocrity as a result. For example, anyone could get you to page 1 of google for the search term "Vets who do bee surgery in the Melbourne CBD on Sunday", but unless that is what your clients use to find you, what's the point? Again, start with your why, set the strategy, and focus the marketing to save time and money.

Another measurement to consider is what is termed your Net Promoter Score. Don't mind the term. This is a basic customer satisfaction measure to see the likelihood of a client "promoting you to another potential client". It can be checked in the form of a survey, a set of smiley faces that the client clicks on after the job, or simply ask after the job "would you recommend us to your friends and family?" There are a few vital reasons to implement a process like this. Firstly, it feels great to get positive feedback. Second, if they will do it, they may refer you on sooner if you ask. Thirdly, and arguably the most important, if you have done a crap job, you need to know to be able to fix it. The most valuable feedback you can get from a client is how to improve your business from their point of view - as long as you action it.

The New Way of Doing Business

# 10

## The World is Small, and Getting Smaller

My parents keep stirring myself and my siblings about the level of international travel we do, both on a professional and personal level. I still remember getting my passport at the same time as my brother and one of my sisters, we were in our mid 20's (ok, I was late 20's, isn't 27 still mid?) and our parents had bought us flights to New Zealand for $99 return. We thought we were the jetsetters back then. Growing up in a small country town we had not been on a plane prior to that. That was 1998.

Fast forward a decade or so. My children had passports before they could talk. They have been overseas at least once every year of their life so far; some years, up to 4 times. One sister was engaged in Venice. The other got married last year in Koh Samui, and of course the whole family went. I now have gold status with both Virgin and Qantas, travelling multiple times a month. We have had staff in the Philippines. My brother in law owns a business with partners in China. My little brother was going to the US regularly for training with his employer. The world is getting smaller and therefore much easier to access, even for a couple of kids from country Victoria. It's weird how fast things have changed, but also pretty cool.

So how does this affect your business? And how will it affect how you do business?

There are positives and negatives. You have access to more clients, and depending on your business the world may be your oyster. Conversely, you are now competing on a global scale. Australia has finally conceded that we cannot efficiently manufacture automobiles. Funnily enough, the way things are going with driverless tech and drones that may not be a bad thing in the near future, but more of my thoughts on that later.

You may now have access to cheaper resources; cheaper product to sell; cheaper raw inputs to make your widgets from. But now so does everyone else. If price is your competitive advantage, you may wish to revisit the strategy section of this book sooner rather than later.

The cost of distribution is also changing. Not only is air travel (and thus freight) getting more competitive, but even on the ground distribution systems are getting a shake-up. Uber is now delivering food to you at your office. Drone technology is being used to make efficient deliveries of low cost goods. I still recall seeing this style of delivery in the movie The Hunger Games, and next moment it's hitting our news feed as reality.

So when was the last time you sat and brainstormed your industry forces and what is next on the radar? This is a massive benefit of the collaboration mentioned previously, where you round up several industry players and have a locked door brainstorm on what's working, what's not and what's next.

Communication is also changing, from the method you use to reach your customers, to how you collaborate with staff, and even how you ensure suppliers are getting your message in a timely and accurate fashion, are all changing. Email was going to change the world, and it seems it's on its way out before some have even got rid of the old fax machine. I encourage you to remove your fax now if you haven't already. We have the latest replacements / alternates with real time chat such as Snapchat and Messenger, direct email "replacements" such as Slack, and of course video such as Zoom and Skype, totally changing the communication landscape.

Admittedly, I have some clients who seem to survive without needing the latest and greatest in communication methods. The laggards who still use cheques, receive the occasional fax from obviously another of the ilk, and convince me at each meeting that this will not change their model. But think about it, when did you last write someone a letter? What portion of bills do you get as email now instead of hard copy? How soon do you pay the email bills compared to the hard copy is also another interesting statistic (it's quicker if you didn't guess)

What you need to do, what the new way of doing business leads you to, is to at least contemplate these changes. Don't burn your email and change to Slack if you don't need to, but at least make a considered decision. Your customers may not even be on Snapchat or Instagram or even Facebook. But at least find out. Because one thing that is guaranteed, is that even if you don't, your competitors will. And the main advantage to business with the world getting smaller, and everyone getting quicker and easier access to everything in the new world of stuff, is that you can build micro-advantage into your business model. Become a little more efficient, constantly, each day better than the previous, and this can help you either gain or retain a competitive advantage. Again, it's doing business on purpose.

How will these global trends, this improved access to all things at the cutting edge of business, affect Joe, the simple suburban plumber?

Remember the software that Joe put in place, to be able to monitor and track his workflow and his employees? He needs a simple and efficient messaging system to be able to constantly communicate with his guys. He could text, but this sounds labour intensive. He could email, but an email trail of 4 or 5 emails gets clumsy, especially if you have to cc more than one person. So he looked at Slack. This allowed him to set up the free app on each of his guys phones, set up what are called channels, and allow each team to have live ongoing records of conversations with each other. And they can keep strictly on topic! They can text each other if they want to catch-up for a beer, but if it is work related, it's on Slack.

Note that I am not promoting Slack as the answer, or even an answer, for your business communication issues. As always, it's a matter of evaluation of your needs and finding a product to suit. And trust me, there is rarely not a product that will suit your needs.

Joe also looked at sourcing some product directly from an overseas supplier. Knowing that he used multiple lots of certain pipe lengths and certain elbow joints, we did the math and worked out buying in bulk shipping container orders of certain products saved thousands a month in supplies. So here was Joe the suburban plumber, now teaching his guys to use cutting edge communication software, state of the art job planning and logistics solutions, and becoming an importer!

The world is getting smaller, and by default easy to play in if you are aware of the tools available to you. If you want to get ahead, and stay ahead, this is the new way of doing business. Surround yourself with the right people, get access to the right tools, and keep a step or two in front of those who don't.

The New Way of Doing Business

# 11

## Is Online Where You Should Be?

When the internet became hot property, back in the early 90's, it was seen as compulsory that you have an online presence. It was not going to just take over business as we knew it; it was going to be the only place to do business. Do you remember Second Life? It still exists but as a shadow of its former self. Every business, big and small, rushed to set up islands and businesses in this virtual world, on the premise that this was the way forward. It wasn't, but there was plenty of cash splashed around in the meantime.

So, looking back, what should our take away be? I'm going to sound monotonous, but check whether a move, online or anywhere, fits your strategy. I'm not here to judge or decide what's right or wrong for your business, simply to ensure you are aware and make educated decisions. There will be opportunities that you could not possibly guess now that may well fit your strategy going forward. It may make sense to pay (if they finally release the ability to market...) to get a Pokémon Go gym set up in your front garden. Maybe you should install VR headsets to allow guided tours of the homes you build. Maybe drone deliveries for your pizzas is a great differentiation strategy. But ensure you at least check that your decisions fit what you want for your business.

Your website is a perfect example of this. Depending on your business and its long term strategy, your online presence could vary from a simple "brochure style" website with your phone number, to a full catalogue with ecommerce, or a full on 3D gaming setup with cutting edge graphics and animations. As always it depends.

Have an eye on what your competitors are doing. Whilst they may have different reasons and a different strategy, they may also allow you to short cut the process (see previous discussion regarding collaboration). Are they evolving an online strategy now? What uses of the latest tech are they playing with? Are there new online competitors popping up to challenge you with newer better product offerings or massive price advantages?

Is it possible for your business to even generate sales online? Or can you at least build a marketing list to reach out to via separate means? Is Facebook a fertile ground for you to find clients, or does your product/service lend itself more to personal touch still? And why?

Joe had already done some work on his online presence so was held in good stead to review and evaluate further options. So it was time for a brain storm. Could we use virtual reality (VR) or augmented reality (AR) to enhance the customer experience? Would people want to book and diarise appointments via our website? With the success of the tap washer video, could we expand to have a series of do-it-yourself videos? How about if the parts needed could be printed by 3D printers? Or delivered by drone from our head office? Could we send robots to complete the job via driverless cars? The possibilities were endless - and mostly impractical for our business. But it was great fun to talk about!

In the end, we decided that the online presence we had was adequate for the time being, and there was lower hanging fruit to pick off first. But, we decided also to have a brainstorming session at least twice per annum, maybe with a drink or two, to fantasise about the latest whiz-bang tech and its application to our business. Maybe a 3D printer and a delivery drone wasn't so far off after all.

# 12

## The Franchise Model, and How it Applies to You

When it comes to looking at business models, it would be remiss to not at least consider the franchise model. In Australia alone there are over 1,000 franchisors with approx. 80,000 franchisee businesses operating. So why is the model so successful?

With a franchise business, the franchisor provides a lot of support in areas that small business operators tend to neglect. They usually have a good brand presence, handle the marketing side to a degree and have market pull when it comes to site locations, hiring staff, etc.

But to my mind at least, the overarching benefit is that a franchise has an established set of systems and procedures in the form of an operations manual so that the business runs without the direct input of the franchisor. You don't wander into McDonalds and still expect Ray Croc to cook your Big Mac for you. He passed away in 1984, but the business did not suffer directly. How would your business handle a similar event?

I speak with a lot of SME owners about succession, and no matter which way they wish to transition their business – sell, franchise, put under management, pass to family members – we always end up at the same place, which is trying to ensure the business operates without their direct input. To do this, there is often a lot of work, but it eventuates in a document or documents that articulate the operation of the business. This operations manual looks remarkably similar to that of most franchisor operation manuals. The reason for that is that it works. Even completing the requirements for ISO accreditation, sometimes needed to win government contracts, goes through a similar process. It's proven, but massively underutilised in the SME business market. How else can you ensure that the business that you have created can continue on in its current state of success, keeping the look, feel and culture that you have enjoyed?

Now the next question – why would you wait, like most do, until the last minute to begin this process? Why not just do it now, and reap the rewards? It's like when you sell a house, and finally get around to tidying up all those annoying handyman bits. Once you finish you want to keep it! Same goes for a business, take the time to do the work now, and reap the rewards sooner rather than later.

And how do you start the process? I'll give you a hint, the answer is found under the heading "Strategy".....

The New Way of Doing Business

# 13

## So, Where to From Here?

OK, so you have made it to the end of the book. Or you cheated and started here. No matter. I wrote this thinking that only my closest friends and family would buy it, and that they definitely wouldn't make it this far in. I had even contemplated filling a few final pages with the Latin text filler that demo books have to show formatting etc., and didn't think anyone would pull me up on it, but I changed my mind.

Having read through the previous chapters, you may have noticed a theme or pattern emerge in regard to what The New Way of Doing Business actually is, and what is involved in implementing the system into your business.

It is an integrated series of actions and thoughts that allow you, the business owner, to run your business on purpose and help it to continue to run itself the same way. It involves setting a strategic plan, starting with the end in mind and keeping this end in focus at all times. It involves sharing the strategy with the team to create a culture of teamwork and success.

It involves setting and maintaining a nimble structure and allowing the scaling of the business, both up and down, as the winds of business dictate. It means keeping close with other players in your industry, collaborating to ensure the whole herd survives any external influences.

It means realising that the knowledge in your head is most likely not exclusive, nor of great value, but the ability use that knowledge, to execute, to plan tactically and make the plan come to reality, is often the most valuable skillset you can develop.

Marketing is not a dirty word, and sharing the awareness of your skills or products is vital to survival, and great marketing can actually trump a great product, but a mix of both is the secret sauce.

Being aware of how customers interact with you, and making this as seamless as possible using the latest appropriate tools and toys to enhance the experience.

So what are the steps? What are you going to do now to ensure that you can maximise your outcomes based on finite resources of inputs?

The best thing you can do is start. This will most likely put you in the front of the pack, as most will not even strike a blow. Depending on your industry, simply being aware of what to do and doing something, anything, may elevate you to market leader.

Don't forget to delegate. This process is much easier if you have the team, if you have a team, on board and aware of what you are trying to do. Remember that delegation is not abdication – you can't simply palm this stuff off to a junior to compile and implement.

Find a reliable third party to be your accountability buddy. Be that a mentor, a business coach, your accountant, your spouse, get someone. It takes time, it takes planning and it takes the desire to succeed. Even when we are brought in to "get it done" there is still a lot of input required from all levels in the business. Having us to push can sometimes help, as it did for Joe, but at the end of the day Joe did it. We just facilitated the process, and ensured that the ship was pointed at the north star for the business. But in the darkest days of business, when it all looks too hard and you want to drop the ball, your accountability buddy can help pull you through.

So, start at the start and go from there. Just don't be the ostrich, with his head buried in the sand, and his butt exposed to the world! And good luck.....

# 14

## Books and Resources

So in following the overall theme of this book, here are some general recommendations based entirely on how I perceived the quality of information or the take away value from each. These may or may not float your boat, and no doubt there are countless other valuable resources out there that I have not even seen or heard of yet. Be that as it may, and in no particular order, I really like:

**Resource**

Entrepreneurs Organisation
> I joined EO in 2014, and it has changed my life. With a focus on the three pillars of business, personal and family, I constantly get out in spades much more than I seem to give. Check them out at eonetwork.org

**Books**

*The 4-hour Work Week* (Tim Ferris)
> A classic tomb that makes you contemplate how your business is structured, how it may be structured, and why you have one in the first place

*The E Myth Revisited* (Gerber)
> Again, a staple read that steps you through the process of systemising and streamlining your business model.

*Scaling up* (Harnish)

> A step by step guide to taking your business to the next level. Aimed more at the medium-large business, the processes are none the less great to implement in a SME if you want to really gain momentum.

*Traction* (Wickham)

> In a similar vein to Scaling Up, but with a simpler implementation method.
>
> For further ideas and updates I also suggest getting in touch with your industry association, network with your peers and engage more regularly with your accountant!

Cheers.

# The New Way of Doing Business

The New Way of Doing Business

www.ingramcontent.com/pod-product-compliance
Lightning Source LLC
Chambersburg PA
CBHW061158180526
45170CB00002B/858